Heath Brougher

A Curmudgeon
Is Born

Heath Brougher

*Bad title for this book.
I'm all about positivity.*

*Enjoy
Heath Brougher*

PUBLISHED BY YELLOW CHAIR PRESS

www.yellowchairreview.com

ISBN-13:978-0692718605 (Yellow Chair Press)
Printed in the United States of America

5606 Fairview Drive
Waco, Texas 76710

Cover Art: Sean Burns

Cover Design: Sarah Moran

"Those thinkers in whom all stars move in cyclic orbits are not the most profound: whoever looks into himself as into vast space and carries galaxies in himself also knows how irregular all galaxies are; they lead into the chaos and labyrinth of existence."

—Nietzsche

CONTENTS

Acknowledgements

"Oil and Water"; "Curriculums"; Evolution of the Fist"; and "A Bouquet of Universes" appeared in *A New Ulster*.

"Yours and Mine" appeared in *Yellow Chair Review*.

"Misperception" appeared in *Eunoia Review*.

"The Reality of Defeatism" appeared in *Maudlin House*.

"Cranial Quakes" appeared in *The Main Street Rag*.

"Not Breastfed" and "Amuck" appeared in *The Angry Manifesto*.

"Jinxed Memories" and "Wooden Wires" appeared in *Fowl Feathered Review*.

"Haphazardly Deliberate" appeared in *Of/ with: journal of immanent renditions*.

"Herd Poisoning" appeared in *VOID Magazine*.

"Prisoners of Patterns" appeared in *Otoliths*.

"Moving Thoughts" appeared in *Mad Swirl*.

"Hello Smithereens" appeared in *Rust + Moth*.

Oil and Water

I haven't been found
of a peaceful mind
in so long if ever truly

I've been always at odds
with the overall masque
the vanity of modern

America with its
Manmade realities
haunting the populace

a society of people
who don't want to
explore their minds

soon enough Thought will be thrown to its death
impaled upon the white picket fences of suburbia.

Curriculums

I am always alwaysing my way through life
      turnstiling through these days
made of illusion and lies

the hamster wheel spinneth eternal

        ...fan rotation and so on...

until I
unlatch from this loop
to see that circular paths are false

for the Truth lives within the Spiral.

to unsnag the grindstone endlessly turning

one must disconnect oneself
in order to stop this massively insane friction.

Yours and Mine

The day is made of slammed doors
     everything is labeled and certain
     and few things are more certain than a slammed door

everything is closed off or separated

the natural boundaries of ownership [wolf piss on a bush]
     have ballooned to a near explosion
        by what Mankind has done to this
extant thing..this thing
     left here for Humanity to find and exploit
to where it has become the dominant force in almost every culture in
the World.

           [these illusions make me sick to my brain]

Misperception

That oak tree

is not really an oak tree.

That oak tree

is only an oak tree

because you call it an oak tree.

Maybe you should stop lying to yourself.

The Reality of Defeatism

Evolution put forth competition

/I am aware of defeat/

competition in almost all facets
of not just human life
but of all life forms in general

however it is especially pronounced
among Mankind which has taken
competition to its Darwinian Apex

a balloon of growing growling conflict
soon enough to explode

/I am aware of defeat/

soon enough all of us will be aware of defeat.

Evolution of the Fist

Violence began as fists fists
turned into swords swords turned
into guns guns turned into nuclear bombs
nuclear bombs turned into masses of dead bodies
evaporated flesh leaving their shadows scorched onto the sidewalk
while the actual viscera just turned to ash.

So what way of inflicting violence comes next?
What insidious weapon comes after the nuclear bomb?

For one must know that Yeat's gyre is still turning
and turning faster with every sinking sun.

A Slant on the Truth

I suppose I'm supposing
eternally.

                       rotational arrest
does not bind me.

very nice sequences
        of sacred geometry
continue to continue
to occur to occur
but what about all the times
these sequences have not occurred?

the Truth is a kite stuck in tree branches
not a thing perfectly afloat the air.

one cannot have all and none simultaneously.

I Feel Sick

I am not at home here;
I am not even at home in this galaxy
Universe
Multiverse?

power lines run above the streets
up with the trees
and I cannot relate to this;

not just the power lines
but the trees;

there is no such thing as natural to me;

I've always been the Eternal Outcast,
the Quiet Weirdo;

my head spins and I enter strange phases of perception
while in the company of others;

the more company
the more disillusionment
at something that is nothing but illusion
which no one else seems to notice or care about;

this is not home; my entire life
has been off-kilter;

Mankind is faced in the wrong direction;

if there is another stage of Sentience
hopefully it will hold the answer

and make some Sense
make some Truth out of all this.

Cranial Quakes

You heard bells like
rumbling tongue-songs spilling
the spit from a hooligan's mouth

a city wind blowback

      ached like a head
when those bell towers tolled
           [told of the plight]

and wicked shards of chime
rode in on the breeze
    to scratch at the skin.

all a loop..........................outta my mind.
this is a pulsar of the nonstop throbbing head.

the Universe is in pain.

Counterclockwise Against the Thorns

After the cacophony
    you calm
        you copasetic yourself
with the concoctions of remedies you cleave to
when the constant clamor
    rings its breath through the air—
    waves, tolls its boisterous brooding through the breeze—
    violently breaching and battering your ears—
hums vibrating into your brain its circular noise
where neurological impulses are battered
and beaten to a bruised state
    of wrecked
        of razed nerves
so recklessly raped as nails
upon a chalkboard.

String of Thought

The thread of thoughts thinkings
the threat of thoughts thinkings,   leaking
hate into the head
            brinking
into sayings

the slither of said sayings
the slaughter of said sayings,   sinking

into the viscera or invading by osmosis the brain.

ears hear arsonist songs sung by anarchist loaves
of Nothingnessism.   F(r)u(i)tility.

Keep a Peeled Eye

You must see the tragedy
atwirl and atwirl and a twirl

the cyclical moon revolves like a sober silver coin

      a loop in a loop of loops which will leave you aloof
   the Truth
      is nowhere
in sight.

the Universe will continue its Universing.

we must remember to keep a sharp peripheral.

Twirl

The shifting   shaping
      shade
          of Proximity
cool breeze of the cosmos
culling Enlightenment
     with every atom
in this whirly dervish swirling
     soup of the Galaxy
          Universe?
          [Multiverse?]
cooings   aggregated clumps
    [less than] crumbs
       of everything
there is   [was?]
          [ever will be?]

Not Breastfed

It is impossible to stifle the short flame
that burns in teardrops and anger until the end.
I am the spark of bad decisions and uselessness
in my own city built of blood and bile.

There were three statues there:
one for nervousness, one for rape,
and one for wisdom—

the one for wisdom had its head cut off.

Jinxed Memories

The shrill and leavened blood
of the immolated children; fire-bones rib-wracked
and squashed brown; now dust
and memory and dream and the uncertainty
of whether these things were ever real,

were ever even made of the Physical Universe
or instead of the lightness of mere fantasy;
a swish and a swirl; a droplet of a galaxy;
the memorial never carved in stone,
never fully knowing if such things ever existed;
the servile mind and memory, lost, limps onward
drowning in the ubiquitous uncertainty that capes all Thought.

A Bouquet of Universes

I do

not exist

which is

a

very strange

paradigm

shift due

to

the fact

that

I am

still

alive.

Prisoners of Patterns

The grotesque cyclical
Nature nurture
has made you all sick
in the head

my spiral screeches against
your symmetry of lies
and circulatory falsehoods
which you've sold yourself into

sewn yourself into
so immensely stitched together
is the fabric and flesh
that it is tremendously difficult
to tear apart
        to tear away from
                to tear off
                    and into the Truth.

Amuck

My God! my gash! I've
never seen a wound of such syphilitic
magnitude than the one you carry in your mind—
a truly poisoned person, not by
the toxic flowers and air, but mangled instead
so deeply by society, hearsay, propaganda—
the confusion machine perplexing the confounded masses—

humans shackled and caged by Technology's easy essence,
amassing, spreading through infection to infection misinformation—
a play upon emotion and any rationale is wiped clearly off
for most people; so this cauldron is stirred
and the disease effects the great populace—

similar to mercury-poisoning, thought-poisoning
swims in phantasmagoric waters; the waves
soon breaching the land, dark waters
and black eyes and minds asleep in permanent limbo,
simple robotic slaves to the talking-moving-picture-screen—

the greatest slave empire Mankind has ever known.

The Lie of the Loophole

They say, "Don't worry.
The scientists will find a loophole
to keep this human race alive."
Loophole— the fakest of false words
in this whole cesspool of the "language of lies."
Nothing new could be born out of a loophole.
The hole would just continue into other loops leading down other
holes.
It would simply be the same regurgitated tactics
already tried and failed. It would mean moving in endless circles.
It would mean there is nothing new to find. It would mean
we weren't even looking.   For Truth to be told
one must sync up to the Great Spiral in order to convey the proper
message.
Not by loophole, but by Spiral will the scientists find a way
to keep this blight of human race alive and kicking, killing.

Haphazardly Deliberate

Mankind has built up like building-blocks
itself into a state of established and set rules—
shackles, constraining the individual to be morphed
into the herd; different geometrical Earthly spots
adorn themselves with varying customs
to keep everyone on the same page so that
a Manmade abstraction of thought
will chain the populace together
with any outsider being picked off—
shunned and shushed and loudly pushed away
so as to no longer interfere with the spurious structure
the masses have built for themselves
without thought and lied into existence—

[insane asylums were founded upon this ideology]

always keeping the community well greased
and running smoothly so they can cuddle within
its warm untruth just like any pack animal,
any herd animal, any extant communal thing,
viruses of course considered and included.

Gravity pulling things together en masse
just as it states in the Rulebook of the Universe.

It's just usually those things are not sentient beings.

Moving Thoughts

The motion of thought
       [pro] motion of thought—
is it good for thought to languish
and lean and loaf
and not leap?

       the brain is a muscle
       slowly turning to blubber
       in this post-postindustrial society,
       this day and age, please
       Science help [but not overly]
       untether all the wrinkles

       the brain weighs a feather
       falls just as fast,
       right Science?

Herd Poisoning

There they are again. Amassed
in their usual vicinity. All in hordes.
Each one so similar to the others.
Indiscernible as blood
in tomato soup.
They worship and follow
coining tradition along the way.

The paths of the hordes
commingle throughout the guts of centuries.
When one horde disagrees with another horde, the trouble begins.
Flesh burns off and war ripples like a California fault-line.
That thought beckoning in the back of minds
for what seems to be forever the question
of integrity and myth.

This is nothing new. It is the usual.

Sometimes doves come
but mostly it's the vultures.

To Sic a Dog

Out through a door a commotion of motion
moving quickly along down the street some fleeting
axiom ran itself out of believers
scripted by fear sneaking a stillness
a million people soon forgetful
now yearning for a fresh contagion
the people once again grow thirsty
and must drink of the vitriolic voice of the dictator
spreading through the office and television
moving shaded by light the clapping crowd
was feeding

it entered the houses guarded by dogs and not
it slipped under the door into hallways
hearing itself on the radio seeing itself embedded
in the brain cavities of the populace
awash the unthinking streamline
it rose from the infested maggot fields
to settle for one last time on the thoughts
where it awaited its turn to be shaken off
every consciousness.

Hello Smithereens

Hello smithereens! the Westerton Bells
have been melted into bullets, so Fascistly unpoetic;
fierce revolving of stars, Rotgutten Karmas;
dysphemism in the chest and head;

I'll never forget you; who could
with that dent you left?

hypoxic illusions moving westward years later
while hoping for a moreleaf clover
finding only diversionary thought patterns
along with the Rosy Retrospection bias and folk intuition
[make no king of me] as the dark cloud moves
bribing viands and villains, manufacturing the outrage,
saying, "you're with Our now,"
with marbles in their mouths
the Kings and Queens of Warshington
have slowly succumbed to this
newly spread American disease.

[everyone is wrong]

The Lovely Vicious Cycle

The only thing
at the end
of this end
of everything
is a nothingness
that is describable

only as
the possibility

of a
new beginning.

I think the Universe was sparked by something else dying.
I think nothing but a new form of Sentience springs from death.

To die a million times is to be reborn a million times.

Wooden Wires

I bleed like boredom.
Everything flows and bleeds through me, not you.
You are the son of the Universe.
You are the son of the Monster.

I put a cork back into the deflating cloud.

You keep growing faces on your head.

I turn into modern.
I turn into a modem.
I turn into moths of math.
I turn into trigonometry.
I turn into Truth.

ABOUT THE AUTHOR

Heath Brougher lives in York, PA and attended Temple University. He is the poetry editor of Five 2 One Magazine. When he is not writing he helps with the charity Paws Soup Kitchen which gives out free dog/cat food to low income families with pets. His work has appeared or is forthcoming in *Diverse Voices Quarterly*, *Chiron Review*, *SLAB*, *Gold Dust Magazine*, *Main Street Rag*, *BlazeVOX*, *Of/with*, *MiPoesias*, *The Angry Manifesto*, *eFiction India*, and elsewhere.

Made in the USA
Middletown, DE
18 October 2016